HerStory

By Anna Wing-Bo Tso
Illustrated by Joanne Lo

Dedication

From Anna Wing-bo Tso: To my mum Mrs Angela Tso, as well as all the niblings who form the next generation of our family tree – Ayumi Horiuchi, Alex Freund, Angelina Freund, Sophia Koo, Edwin Koo, Elise Chu, Charlotte Tso and Mai Chi Law.

From Joanne : To my mum Connie, my aunt Mary, Franklin, Amy Lo and all the faboulous women out there!

Acknowledgements

We feel very honoured to have received great support from readers, libraries, and community organizations ever since we published the first book of *Hong Kong Stories* (2017 -). First and foremost, we wish to express our particular thanks to Alpha Academic Press for publishing our books, our deepest gratitude to Sunrise Charitable and Education Fund for sponsoring the book series, and our big thanks to Tai Po Pubic Library for giving us a chance to introduce our picture books to parents and children in the library's public talk in December 2018. We are also obliged to Ms Morgan Davies, teacher librarian of the American School Hong Kong, who invited us to give 'meet-the-author' book talks and 'meet-the-illustrator' workshops to international school children in February 2019. We are grateful too to Lieutenant Winnie Ho of Hong Kong Air Cadet Corps (HKACC), who arranged a family storytelling session for our new book, *Herstory* (2019), at the Hong Kong Aviation Club in March 2019. Last but not least, we must thank the readers who love and voted for *Culinary Charades* (2017) in the Golden Dragon Book Awards hosted by the Association of Librarians in English Speaking Schools (ALESS). Without their warm support, our debut would not have been shortlisted as a finalist for the 2019 Debbie Alverez Memorial Award, the only children's choice picture book award in Hong Kong.

Foreword

You won't fully appreciate the magnitude of what your parents have done for you until you are a parent yourself.

Growing up with Wing Bo and the rest of the gang of cousins in Hong Kong in the golden 80's was a bliss. We saw one another almost every Saturday at grandma's - the kids mucking around, the adults chatting about adult things. To me, Aunty Angela (大舅母) is forever the Aunty who can cook the best, look after the grandparents the best, and care for all the big and little children with the most care and attention. I never really 'know' her. Kids just don't care much about what their older relatives are like. It takes four decades and *Herstory* for me to gain a glimpse of what Aunty Angela is like, which also helps explain a lot about why her children are all accomplished in many ways.

Mothers of this generation talk about striving for this mystical 'balance' – the balance between family and career, the balance between 'me-time' and 'kids-time', an almost utopian, unachievable 'life balance'. As a mother of two myself, having a clinical doctorate degree, being a holder of a university academic position, working as a clinical specialist, and starting my own business (plus a PhD), I have to accept that the notion of finding a perfect balance is impossible. I'm watching my son having his swimming lesson as I'm writing this! So how did the previous generation of mothers do it, and did it so well that all of my cousins are outstanding contributors to society in many ways? I think I've found part of the secret in *Herstory*.

One time I've heard a child psychiatrist said - the only important thing about parenting is to give your children unconditional love. I don't know much about the modern application of the complicated term 'feminism', but *Herstory* made me think and appreciate my mum and many women in the previous generations even more. Like Aunty Angela, with her abilities and talents, options and opportunities, she used her strength, power, and determination to choose and act on what is most important to her. To me, that is true feminism.

From Adelaide with love,
Dr. Wendy Cheung
Mum of Alex and Angie

Before I start sharing my story with you, I have a few words for those who think there is something wrong with the book title: no, 'herstory' is neither a typo nor a spelling mistake. Derived from the word 'history', 'herstory' is a word coined in the late 20th century, which refers to (1) history written not by men but by women, and (2) history about women. In this story, I shall do both - you are going to read how a woman recounts true stories of an amazing woman in her family.

For hundreds and thousands of years, Chinese women have never been recorded properly in traditional Chinese genealogy (族譜), nor have they been featured prominently in children's books written in English. To do justice, let's bring Chinese women back to centre stage.

When I was a small kid, my favourite past time was to visit the library with my mom, Angela and my elder brother, Andrew. Shortly afterwards, my younger brother, Angus also joined us. The four of us often took the green-top minibus to get to the City Hall Library in Central, which was the largest public library in Hong Kong in the 1980s. Each time, we would spend the whole afternoon browsing bookshelves, discovering and reading interesting books until dusk. There was no required reading, no homework nor book reports to work on, and no hurry at all. Our mom made us see that reading books is about enjoyment.

As a book lover, mom has a decent book collection at home too. She kept buying her kids books as presents, and occasionally, comic books as well. I can still recall the pleasurable moments when she read to us sad orphan stories written by Charles Dickens and Mark Twain. I also remember how Andrew and I kept reading and discussing the comic version of Mary Shelley's *Frankenstein* and Herman Melville's *Moby-Dick*.

Wild imaginations unleashed by these readings were unstoppable. My young mind desired more, and I couldn't help going through mom's bookshelves, wanting to read every one of her favourites. But not all her books were easy to read. Homer's *Iliad*, Aeschylus' *Eumenides*, and Cao Xueqin's *The Dream of the Red Chamber* on her bookshelves were just too challenging.

Mary Shelley's *Frankenstein*

In order to unlock the mysteries in her books, I chose English and Comparative Literature as my majors at university. Though my choice was indeed my own, I am grateful for the eye-opening experiences she brought to me.

Herman Melville's *Moby-Dick*.

I most certainly would not have become an associate professor teaching English language and literature had my mom not introduced her world of books to me, which totally blew my mind. Yet perhaps the one who has been truly influenced by mom's foreign language book collection is my younger brother, for Angus now works overseas in a German giant company that has a growing network of over 2,000 locations across 140 countries around the world. You see, learning foreign languages is the key to an international future.

Mom's book series on Western fine arts had made a permanent impact on Andrew too. Andrew first developed his passion in art through appreciating paintings such as Van Gogh's "The Starry Night" and Matisse's Goldfish. His art sense grew stronger as mom let him learn sketching and drawing in a fine art gallery in the neighbourhood. He ended up practicing the profession of architecture, founding his privately owned architectural firm, which has designed-built such architect-led construction projects as hotels, shopping arcades, bars and pubs, apartments, and chapels in South East Asia.

"But you are a registered nurse? Most people who grew up in the Hong Kong education system turn out to be open to science and closed off about art, or vice versa. You are good at both. And how come you have collected so many books about literature and fine art? Tell me, mom." I could not see through it.

picasso

"Firstly, I have to thank my mother, who sent me to the Sacred Heart Canossian College. The college used to locate in Caine Road of the Hong Kong Island. The trip to school was long, but I felt privileged because my teachers were excellent, in particular my fine art teacher, whose name is also Angela, coincidentally." Mom's eyes shone brighter as she mentioned her school days.

"Angela showed us the key to Western fine art and high culture. Inspired by her teaching, I obtained good grades in my matriculation and I got admitted to the Department of Fine Art of the Chinese University of Hong Kong (CUHK)." Her flashback continued.

"But I didn't want to burden my parents with my university tuition fees, so I turned down the offer at CUHK and joined the nursing school, the jolliest years of my life. And you know the rest of the story." Mom explained with a smile.

Yes, I do know the rest. After graduating from the nursing school, she became a registered nurse. Her outstanding performance impressed her supervisor in the ward, thus soon, she was recommended to further her training in England, which was actually a promotion offer. Yet because of her love for her family, mom declined the golden opportunity. Then some years later, she gave up her career entirely to take care of her three small children.

For her parents, her Mr. Right and her children, she willingly gave up her studies, her promotion opportunity, and then her career without the slightest hint of hesitation or regret.

I don't know what the feminists would say about this, but this is her story, and I am proud of my mom, my muse.

Book series author

Anna Wing-bo Tso is an associate professor of English and Comparative Literature at The Open University of Hong Kong. Interested in children's literature, gender studies, language arts and translation studies, Anna has published books, chapters and research articles in peer-reviewed journals across Asia, Europe, the U.K., the U.S., Canada, Australia and New Zealand. Her recent publications includes *Academic Writing for Arts and Humanities Students* (McGraw-Hill, 2016), *Teaching Shakespeare to ESL Students* (Springer, 2017), and *Digital Humanities and New Ways of Teaching* (Springer, 2019). In her free time, she also writes and publishes plays, poems, short stories, and children's picture books for leisure. Her prose and verse have appeared in literary periodicals and national newspapers, including *The Font, American Tanka, New Academia,* and *China Times*.

Book series illustrator

Joanne Lo was born in Canada and raised both in Toronto and Hong Kong. Having grown up and living on a beautiful outlying island called Cheung Chau, she has a special love for nature, animals, art and one's spiritual growth. She began her career in creative media since graduating from university majoring in Cultural Studies and Visual Studies. She is the illustrator of *Teaching Shakespeare to ESL Students* (Springer, 2017), a book housed in the Yale and Harvard University Libraries and downloaded for over 11,628 times since its publication.

Hong Kong Stories
The Complete Series

Tailor-made for young readers at ages 8 - 12 in Hong Kong and beyond, the *Hong Kong Stories* series is a collection of English stories written with the local Hong Kong context in mind. Ideal for language learning, leisure and reading aloud among readers young and old, the book series brings together original short stories and pictures about various aspects of Hong Kong's everyday life:

Book 1: *Culinary Charades*, a taster of Hong Kong food
Book 2: *The Summer of 1997*, a walk down memory lane in Hong Kong
Book 3: *Unforgettable Neighbours*, a Hong Kong animal safari
Book 4: *Taming Babel*, the serendipity of the Cantonese language
Book 5: *Herstory*, a tribute to Hong Kong women
Book 6: *A Tale of Two Haunted Universities*, a spooky Halloween treat

www.ingramcontent.com/pod-product-compliance
Lightning Source LLC
Chambersburg PA
CBHW041215240426
43661CB00012B/1051